Ordinary Trauma

By Brian Rihlmann

©®

"The Type"

I told a friend a story
about a former coworker
who left work early one day
and never returned

two days later
when I walked in the warehouse door
someone shoved a newspaper
in my face
pointed and said
"Read this!"

he'd been arrested
he'd pimped his 14 year old step daughter
in motel rooms all over town
and filmed it too

with her face pinched
my friend asked
if he'd seemed the type
and I said not really
but do they ever?

and the ones that do seem
"the type"
usually aren't
but sometimes they're transformed
into monsters anyway
by virtue of a face
they didn't choose
or habits that seem
outside the norm

turned into "types"
by the unacknowledged shadows

of good and beautiful people
that slithered out
from between the slats
of their white picket fences

8 Hours Of Happy Place

At dusk I step outside
with a bowl of yogurt
to watch the day's last colors fade
and as I swallow vanilla sweetness
I watch one of the Tongan women
who works at the adult daycare
in the house next door
leading a woman inside
for the night

she swings her legs, stiff-kneed
moans and shakes her fists
the big woman puts an arm around her
says "I know....we'll go tomorrow, ok?"
then they go inside

everyone wants to go somewhere
somewhere else
that makes them happy, I suppose
I wonder where that place is
for her

the last pink clouds
have gone to grey
my spoon scrapes the empty bowl

I go inside
climb into bed
hope for eight hours
of uninterrupted
happy place

19

I was 19 in 1993
living on my own
in a tiny studio apartment

my girlfriend and I
had split
or rather, I had,
to chase some crazy bitch
who seemed more interesting

it hadn't worked out
she turned out to be
a bit too interesting

how restless I'd get
on the weekends
between the hated 9 to 5

I'd pedal my bike
all over the city
because there was nothing else to do

I couldn't drink at bars
and pick up women
that way yet

but I found a corner store
that didn't I.D.

beer at night and TV
and the bike on weekends
got me through

I guess it can be
a good experience

to feel stuck
trapped

everyone should feel that way
once or twice

I wonder if the kids
growing up now
will ever have it

they'll never know
the desperation of
being stuck in a room
waiting for the phone to ring
because you can't miss
her goddamn call

now you can check
all your social media
dating profiles
and messenger apps
and ONE of them
is bound to throw you a crumb
to keep you going

it's a different kind of stuck—
we're stuck everywhere
instead of in one place

we float through cyberspace
like asteroids knocked out of orbit
and escape the gnaw that way

I'd like to say
that the kind of stuck
I knew as a young man
was worse...

more lonely, agonizing
and soul-forging
than this dissipation

but I'm not so sure
about that

and now I too
swipe and tap
through 2 a.m. agony
instead of stepping outside
to drink another beer
and smoke

watch the moths
dance in dusty cones of lamplight
listen to the alley cats
fight or fuck
somewhere in the darkness

from the sound alone
you can't tell

99 Blank Pages

The first page of the notebook
that I write these words in
is dated 3/5/17
and reads:

"This will be my new
sobriety/ gratitude journal
after another two week bender..."

and I go on
about what caused
my relapse (bullshit!)
and what my plan is
this time (more bullshit)

then I list several things
I'm grateful for
one of which
was the job I had
a job I hated, hated, hated
a job I drank myself stupid
trying to forget
every single night

the entry ends there
followed by 99
pristine white pages

99 pages
of blackouts
of round the clock boozing

99 pages of misery
and bloated sickness
for which I am entirely grateful—

as I finally hit
that fabled "rock bottom"
that allowed me
to stand up again
and quit for good
on September 12, 2017

sometimes
this
is how it goes

A Burning Fucking Man

soon they'll swoop
and descend
on our fair city
our "Biggest Little City"
in VW busses
old motorhomes
and rented box vans
strapped with fat tire bicycles
camping gear
barbecue grills....

looking like first world refugees
fleeing the crushing banality
of their daily lives

they'll swarm our streets
and highways
our airport
our supermarkets
they'll empty the beer coolers
and ice machines

they'll clog the arteries
of this town
like a cheap casino
steak and egg breakfast

perhaps if I owned
a business
a liquor store
a sporting goods store
or a marijuana dispensary

I might be happy
about your arrival here

but I don't
and I'm not

and I have no interest whatsoever
of ever joining
tens of thousands of you
out on the playa
to watch the burning
of the man

i am
a burning
fucking
man

A "Can Do" Sorta Guy

He was a "can do" sort of guy.
Ex-military. West Point.
Clean shaven, and with the
"high and tight." All that.
And yes, he did walk
as though he had the proverbial
"stick up his ass."

He'd fly in every couple of months
and walk the aisles of the warehouse,
chatting with the rank and file
about safe subjects,
things he'd gleaned about us
through casual conversation.

Since I had no kids,
and no interest in NASCAR,
football, or politics,
he had a tougher time with me.

And on that day I cringed
when I saw him turn the corner
and head towards me.

After I'd shrugged
and mumbled my way through
several questions, he asked,
"What's the matter?"

I took a chance.
You never knew...
maybe he had an answer.

"I'm depressed." I said.

His brow furrowed,
deeper than any brow
I'd seen before,
and probably since.

"You're depressed?"

I nodded.

He stared at me for a moment longer,
like Kafka's cockroach,
or as though
I'd just sprouted a second head
from the side of my neck,
then did a crisp about face,
and marched off.

I listened as the click of his heels
vanished into the low buzz
of the overhead lights.

Then I hopped back
onto my forklift,
laid my head
on the steering wheel,
and wondered how many hours
til that first drink.

A 90 Pound Ton

all 90 pounds of her
was never
a small thing
not the times
she pinned me down
head flung back
and nails dug in

and not tonight
as I lie here
eyes open
the weight of her
still on my chest
and I can't breathe

perhaps in another life
when I'm successful
with a big house like his
in the foothills
overlooking the city

we'll sit on the back deck
on summer nights
sip champagne
gaze at the lights shining below
and say—
what a view!

A Dairy Farm

I visited a dairy farm once
I remember how they shoved the cows
through the metal gates
through a labyrinth of fences
how they cursed and kicked them
to get them moving

they hooked plastic tubes
to shriveled udders
sucking them dry
as a machine
pumped and hissed
in the background

I thought of that today
as I drove the freeway
at a crawl
amid blaring horns
through a lane shift
and bottleneck
on the way to somewhere
I didn't care to go

A Double, At Least

I grabbed the bat
from beneath the bar
and brandished it, yelling
"That's enough, assholes!
I've already had a gun
pulled in here tonight!"

They stopped shoving,
but the three hundred pounder
with the shaved head
glared at skinny me, shouted,
"Fuck you, motherfucker!
I ain't afraid of your bat!"

I blinked. Glared back. Waited.
His friends talked to him,
sat him down, got him a drink.

Not the reaction I expected,
but at least I'd smoothed the wrinkles
from the rest of the night.

Under the counter,
the bottle clinked
against the glass
as I poured myself
a vodka cranberry.
Double, at least.

A Good Girl

I met her online
and she said
she wished
her boyfriend
would treat her
like a proper whore—

tie her up
spank her
pull her hair
fuck her hard
fuck her in the ass

everyone thinks
I'm such a good girl
she said

we chatted for weeks
talked a lot of shit
but never met
and though she never sent a photo
I imagine she looks
a bit like this woman
in a navy-blue business suit
sitting with her boyfriend

he dutifully brings her coffee
then kisses her
gently on the lips
and walks to the bathroom

she glances at me
several times
crosses her legs
under a skirt
that just won't stay down
no matter how she tries

A Google Earth Poem

this night has plans for me
other than sleep
and as Missouri's on my mind
I go there in a virtual way
with finger swipes
on the looking glass
that lead me
down the 3-D streets of Springfield
the images just real enough
for each building
to cast a spell

I see the neighborhood grocery
the corner store
the pizza joint
and the warehouse
I worked all those twelve
and fourteen hour shifts in

I see the bars
where I drank myself numb enough
every weekend
to forget that Monday exists
and the bars I later drank in
to both forget about
and remember you

I pinch out
fly high and hover
hesitate as I hold America
between my thumb and middle finger
then I dive bomb back in
on our old apartment building

these photos were taken
in the fall
the swimming pool
is covered
and the maples
are starting to turn

I can see oil stains
in the parking lot
and the balcony
where we sat
on summer nights
pretending it was right
hoping it might last
long enough
that we'd break through
and be in the clear

I roam the city
and wonder
if it's good for me
to crack this open
to peer across
space and time this way
but I go ahead
cuz good's got nothing
to do with it

A Knock At My Door

how he found my apartment
I didn't know
but there came a knock
and suddenly 6 foot 6
and 300 pounds
of meth fueled fury
stood at my door
looking for a guy
and was he here?
had I seen him?

past the boa constrictor of fear
that squeezed my neck
I forced the words through
"No, man....I haven't...."

he went on
telling me the whole story
about how that little punk
had stolen his car
and "I know his cousin
is your roommate, man
so if you see that motherfucker...
kick him to the curb!"

I thought about the story that he—
most likely cowering
in the back bedroom—
had given me...
this maniac had ASKED him
to steal his car
and they were gonna split
the insurance money

maybe this maniac

had changed his mind...

well, he finally went away
after about my fifth reassurance
that I hadn't seen this dude

I shut the door
locked it
and breathed

then walked back
to the bedroom
where he practically
got on his knees
to thank me

"You gotta go."
I said
"Give it five minutes
then go out the fucking window.
Don't come back."

his cousin
my roommate
was pissed
but I didn't give a shit

A Knot Of Cringe

about 15 years ago, it was
as my spiky haired friend and I
staggered to the next pub
during a crawl in downtown Springfield

we drifted through the crowd
stepped over the puke
ogled the college girls
and avoided the usual zealots
with hand painted verses on sandwich boards
reminding us of our drunken and sinful ways

until we passed a man
standing silently on a street corner
holding a six foot wooden cross

after a moment
my friend yelled
I turned to see him posing before it
arms outstretched
head hung
tongue lolling out

then he laughed
skipped along the sidewalk
and rejoined me
as I forced a chuckle
to mask a massive knot of cringe

A Rapture Of One

do you realize
how often you visit me?
don't your coworkers wonder
where you've gone?
do they think it's the rapture?

does he ever reach for you
and find you gone
then climb out of bed
to roam the house
and whisper your name?

does he step outside
into the muggy firefly night
to call to you
and then return
with a knot in his belly so deep
only to find you snoring softly
on your side of the bed?

half a continent away
I awaken
to thrash in the sheets
to reach for my pillow
to clutch it
and try to sleep

A Second Heartbeat

i came home from work
and walked in on you
dancing naked
in front of our bedroom mirror
and you screamed
and covered yourself
but then laughed
because it was just me

i should have laughed with you
and grabbed you
and thrown you onto the bed

but I just turned and walked out
went into the bathroom
closed the door
and sat on the toilet awhile
my head in my hands

because how can you laugh
or fuck
or even smile
when you're being raped
by life and grinding 12 hour shifts
surrounded by concrete
and cardboard
and people you can't stand

and the only thought you have
is of running far far away

it throbs in your brain
like a second heartbeat

A Subject To Avoid On Thanksgiving

Today is for feasting, football,
and drinking ourselves stupid,
and, as the evening progresses,
someone will pull the pin,
with something like:

"I think he's doing a great job!"
Or...
"I think he sucks!"

and it will clatter noisily
to the floor
in the ensuing,
openmouthed silence.

A dozen spotlights
with dilated pupils
will blaze upon the red
or blue sheep of the family
who dared utter
such blasphemy.

And the trial will begin,
like a slow motion
grenade explosion
beginning with,
"Explain yourself!"
ending with shrapnel shouts
of "Idiot!"
and gavel fists
pounding the table
until the glasses spill
and the Cabernet
stains the white tablecloth
that belonged to grandma.

Maybe it'll wash out,
but I wouldn't bet on it.

A Stationary Light

he showed me
how sound traveled
at a certain speed

"you see how he hit the ball
and the sound took a moment
to reach us?"

I nodded
I understood

later, I learned
in an astronomy book
that light was like that too
only faster

I'd flip my bedroom light
on and off
and try to catch it
in the act

but I've never understood
how other things—
the tectonic shifts that happen
between hearts
or inside one

how it is
that the light
from those cataclysms
never reaches our eyes

it must be there
but the shadows
are all we see

A Strange Message

outside the window
of the south branch library
where I like to sit
there are rooftops now
between me and the mountains
that weren't here the last time I was

(it's progress, Brian, progress...
jobs and all that good shit)

while I absorb
this new affront
to my mile-wide streak
of hermetic misanthropy—
so help me—
a woman walks by
carrying a skunk
under her arm

she sees me watching
gives a quick half smile
then hurries along

I sit here
scratch my stubble
like Freud
mulling over
a difficult dream

I look up again
from writing this
to see her return
carrying a large snake

I pinch myself
I am, in fact,
awake

finally I get up
follow the sound of voices
into another room

It's a show
they're putting on
for the kids

of course...

and here I thought
it was some kind of message
from the universe

I'm glad it wasn't
I'm never very good
with those

Aftershocks

by definition
aftershocks are less severe
less damaging

I wonder about that
I wonder how that can be
when they go on and on

when over and over
I am knotted
with each tremor

I shiver at the aftershocks
like I never did
before the main event

I was merely surprised
at how quickly
it all collapsed

All Useless

in the dream
a field burns
and instead of fleeing
all the mice
and other creatures
all the meek
and tiny dirt dwellers
run into the flames

a phalanx of them
shoulder to shoulder
races into hot death
burning like Buddhist monks

above
the hawks and eagles
circle in confusion
and cry out

the glorious plumage
the wide wingspans
the fearsome talons
all useless now

they survey
the scorched earth below
then turn their pitiless eyes
on one another

An Advancing Army

it's monday
and all across america
we stand in the cold
outside office buildings
and warehouses
shuffling our feet
waiting for someone
to unlock the door

or sit in break rooms
drinking coffee
and waiting to punch the clock
our lips as grimly sealed
as the grey winter sky
or forcing smiles and small talk
but all with the same
bewildered eyes
wondering
how how how
goddamn it
is it monday already...
and where did the weekend go?

all those Sunday evening glances
at the clock
and counting the hours left
til bedtime
or the morning alarm
as though we could catch it
in the act
with its thieving little hands
in the cookie jar...

useless

and then awakening at 2 a.m.
and again at 3
hearing faintly
the clomp of boots
of an advancing army
conquering our territory
piece by piece

An October Maple In July

he walks by
smacking a fresh pack of smokes
against his palm
and as he passes
within ten feet of a trash can
peels the cellophane and the foil
lets them flutter to the ground
carefree as an October maple in July

these strange and rebellious leaves
glitter as they catch the morning sun
thousands, millions of them
much too haughty
to ever become mere soil again

And Yet

at some point
I became nailed
to his same cross
where he's hung above them
in petty martyrdom
since I can remember
and from that vantage said
look at them—
this is undone!
and that isn't right!

so soft were the nails
so gentle the hammer blows
I didn't even notice
as they were driven in

but they're there now
I see myself
as though from a distance
and it seems like
I could wiggle free
if I tried, and yet...

Another One?

Things are definitely fucked,
when you read the headline
and your only thought is,
"Shit...another one?"

And you don't read the article,
because you know the story
like a bad song stuck on repeat.

How everyone in the place
thought it was firecrackers
or a car backfiring
but quickly realized it wasn't,
and then screamed and ran,
ducking and hiding
in corners and under tables,

while some of the bullets
shattered glass,
and some found flesh,
and the sacrificial blood ran
dark on the floor,

and then one final shot
found its target,
the target
that was the goal
right from the start,

the dead and bleeding bodies
only incidental,
a way to build up to it,
to summon courage
like a better man would have
with whiskey,

like they used to -

a bottle,
and a loaded pistol,
sitting in the bathtub
listening to sad songs
on the radio.

Don't you guys
do it that way anymore?

Instead, you drag children down
with you into inescapable darkness
to force your own hand,
because how can you
face the world after this?

Now you can do it...
and it almost seems easy.

Anyone Got A Pen?

not 15 minutes of fame
Mr. Warhol
but 15 minutes
of the illusion
thereof

this jewel
is all ours

I wonder
will the burning earth
with its bloody
tearful history
seem famous
to the swollen sun

perhaps dark matter
will recoil in horror
from the spectacle
of this blue speck
swallowed

perhaps the coronal flames
will ask an autograph
from the soil
from the boiling seas
from the strange animals
that have succeeded us

but alas—
where's a pen
when you need one?

At 50 Dollar Motels

in the early morning
people walk their dogs
on the trampled grass
and leave offerings for the flies

smokers puff
in the breezeways
and suck down
the free watery coffee
two-fisted
from tiny styrofoam cups

we walk downstairs
to check our vehicles
nod hello as we pass
but glance over our shoulders
with narrowed eyes

everyone seems a bit shady
rumpled and haggard
from half-sleeping
amidst strange noises
and the night's rolling journey
across unfamiliar hollows
and coiled springs

we pace the corridors
yawn and rub sand from our eyes
as we remember where we are
where we're headed
and why

Bar Brawl Enlightenment

you may sit
in the lotus position
for a lifetime
and never get it
but nothing brings enlightenment
quite like a head butt
to the face
when you are dead drunk
a blow which nearly
knocks you cold
and you see the stars
everyone talks about

then having to fight your way
from your hands and knees
back to your feet
while a crowd kicks
and punches you
only to be grabbed
around the neck
and choked half unconscious
by the muscular arm
of the bouncer
who releases you
when he feels the blood
from your broken nose
pouring hot over his skin

after that
you know something
about the world
that you didn't know before

Be Grateful Your Anxiety Brings Laughter To The World

on your worst days
you try the techniques:
the rationalizing
the mindfulness
the breathing

you build a dam
of tongue depressors and Elmer's glue
against a thick stinking river of sewage

when someone slams that door
yet again
that you've asked them not to slam

you growl and show your teeth
and they walk off
muttering
"What's his problem?"

but there's no way
to answer that
you've tried...

and they heard every word—
as a punchline

Bible Scholar

I got interested
in the Bible
when I was around
7 or 8 years old
not sure why...

we had one at home
dusty and musty
sandwiched between
other untouched books
on a shelf

I'd open it at random
and read a little
flip through the pages
like a comic book

the words were strange
they didn't sound
like people talked
but I tried

there were lots
of "begats"
and battles
and bloodshed

that episode in the garden...
god was pissed
at those two

and that Job fellow
poor bastard
I thought:
no one deserved that

finally I lost interest
put it back on the shelf
not understanding things
any better than before
but with lots of questions
inchoate

they grew like ghostly weeds
through the garden
of my young mind
a million flowers
in tight buds
waiting to burst

Black Feet

a block away
I see him
laid out on the sidewalk
ankles crossed
dark skinned feet
protruding from grey sweatpants
a black man
I think

half a block
and I say, no
a pair of black socks
threadbare

closer still
I'm wrong again
bare feet
a white face
inside a drawn hoodie

I pause nearby
he breathes
snores
alive

an empty bottle
beside him

as I walk on
I wonder
how many empties
it took

how far from that
was I

and how long
out on the street
for pale skin
to get that color

Blackberry Bush

It almost felt like mine
as every morning
I watched the leaves unfurl

then came the buds
the little white flowers
and after the bees did their work

clusters of tiny green globes
appeared, that by fall
would sweeten and darken

then the landscapers came
and inside the office
I blared Judas Priest through my headphones

to drown out the hedge trimmers
hacking their way through the bushes
on that side of the building

and at lunchtime
I ate inside for a change
afraid to see what they'd done

Bloodline Roulette

Every nice and normal family
has it's stories,
those dark stains
on the hardwood
under that beautiful rug.

They drift to young ears
as you wander
among the grownups knees
at gatherings
and holiday parties.

About an uncle in prison,
and a long dead grandfather
who tried killing grandma
and the kids with the car
after a bad day at work.

A cousin who became a drunk
and lived in flophouses
and camped under bridges
until he vanished
and all they found
were empty bottles,
but no body.

And there was talk
of a nervous breakdown or two,
which would explain those times
I locked myself in my apartment
until it was safe to come out.

I somehow avoided prison,
never tried murdering
any of my girlfriends

(though I wanted to),
and,
miraculously,
set the bottle down.

Things are relatively calm,
these days.

But they flow through me,
those people I never knew,
tickling my veins
like itching powder
with grey ghostly fingers
and I wonder...

are they pooling deep
swelling some hidden reservoir
until the dam bulges,
and bursts,

or awaiting some trigger
to crank open the spillways
and flood through me
cackling in mad
and bloody rebirth.

Because you never know
how many drops of them
are flowing through you,

until you
just
know.

Bristlecones

Is it any more strange
than believing
that a man rose from the dead
that wine becomes blood
for me to believe
that just by being
among you—

you twisted, gnarled
sentinels of the desert
sprigs when pharaohs
were helpless babes
midlife as Rome crumbled—

that I may absorb
a sliver
of your endurance
your willingness
to go on, despite
all you have weathered
all you have seen?

Busted

she smiles at me
as she sits down
at a table facing mine
jeans and t-shirt

but here's another
walking by
click of stilettos
short skirt

she stands
hips cocked
one arm akimbo
like she's working the corner

she sees me
and turns away
points her bubble ass
in my direction

I look back
toward the first
towards chipped ice eyes

a smile gone
as the rising steam
from my hour-old coffee

Can You See Me Pee-ing?

a bunch of us
were drunk at the river
jumping off the dead man's cliff
(a fifty footer)
and doing backflips off the rope swing
when my pal Joey
stood in the green water
up to his waist
and did a slow twirl
with his arms outstretched
while singing
"Can you see me pee-ing?"
for the entertainment of all of us
on the riverbank

we couldn't stop laughing

I think of that today
as I stand on this empty beach
and let loose a stream—
not too close
but still within sight
of some cliffside houses
with big windows
facing the sea

and I'm compelled to sing to them
if they're watching
"Can you see me pee-ing?"

then I start to laugh
and shake
and I dribble
all over my shoes

fuckin' Joey, man...

Casting Our Nets

On New Year's Eve,
a young woman writes in the sand
with a stick of washed up driftwood
faded white as bone:

"Joy"
"Love"
"Empowered"

and then lets the ocean
pull the words into her depths,
as though casting a net
to draw from the universe
the desired things themselves.

I remember writing our names
on a beach somewhere,
inside a heart,
with the word "forever,"

and how we stood
on the cliff above,
looking down on it,
wrapped in each other's arms.

The waves took that, too.

You know
how this ends.

Maybe I should tell her about that,
but she probably read about
this inscribing-hopes-in-the-sand technique
in some bestselling book,
and I am just a nosy guy
walking alone on a beach.

Cataracts

inside
a caricaturist
runs loose
drawing enemies
drawing friends
on my walls
with mad abandon

if you could see
his portrayals
you'd say
"that looks nothing like me!"

you become a cherub
or a gargoyle
a demon or angel
Madonna or whore

sometimes I stare
too long at his art
it clouds my vision
like cataracts
between you and me
between me and me

Comparison Is Not Always The Thief Of Joy

We sit stage-side
as flesh too old,
pale and flabby
jiggles under lights
too bright.

She gyrates her hips,
humping the brass pole
as she slides down into a squat,
looks at me and smiles.

A front tooth missing.
I look away,
slap a dollar on the stage anyway.
Good flexibility.
I gulp my whiskey shot,
wash it down with beer.

Then, a scraping sound
and a crash makes me turn.
Two groups face off, mostly men,
but a couple of women too.

A table's been overturned,
and they're shoving and yelling.

One woman lunges
at another, screaming,
grabbing handfuls of hair.

The dancer on stage
leaps off, pendulous tits
swinging as she runs
across the room, shouting
"Don't you touch her!"

I'd asked my buddy earlier,
"Why did you drag me here?"

Now, as he watches the scuffle,
this Jerry Springer moment,
he leans back in his chair,
smiles and says,
"Man, I look at shit like this
and my life doesn't seem so bad."

Dead Weight

Certain hopes
must be shed
and allowed to sink,
before their dead weight
drags us down
to shadowy trenches.

Like the hope
that i will grow
shark skin
that your barbed hooks
cannot pierce,
that it will enfold
and dissolve
the rusty ones
already dangling.

That my wounds
will ever completely close,
and salty currents
cease to sting,
cold ones cease to chill.

That storms will
regain their senses,
and no longer
darken the horizon,
nor churn the seas
till waves
clash in angry battle.

Or that my eyes
will ever adjust
to the dim light
of the murky waters

in which we swim,
and grant me more
than mirror flash moments
of understanding.

Death Of A Fawn

a blood trail follows
to where her body lies
roadside, twisted

dragged by hooves
by hands that seconds before
held the murderous wheel

at my slow approach
a thousand blue-green flies
rise to cloud the air
brilliant in the light

a writhing mass
of their progeny
fills her open mouth

just as
the sour milk stench
fills my lungs
my veins

I pause
gaze at the hole
where her eye had been
black as mother's grief
staring into the sun

Denial Deep As The Lines On His Face

his knees are scabbed
from last week's fall
at least he didn't bloody
his nose this time
like the night
I helped him up
off the floor

it's vertigo the doctor said
a CAT scan showed nothing

and did you mention
the case of beer a day
you pour into your skinny body?

this, I don't ask

I've already thrown it out there:
"I'll go with you
to an AA meeting
if you want"

he looked at me
nodded slowly

the deep lines on his face
are those a man
ten years older

tonight
there's a sixer
in the fridge
instead of an 18 pack

I've tried that strategy too

Do Not Fret

Do not fret—
the balled-up pages
the torn trashcan pages
the angry ashen pages
the inky black smoke

of Shakespeare
of Wordsworth
of Whitman
of whoever

were also filled with things
that would make you cringe

just as they
just as we
are filled
with balled up
torn, angry
half-burned
half-swallowed
half-digested pages

a crumpled mass
that groans
deep in our bellies

and always will

Don't Be Surprised

No one should be surprised
in a land that glorifies money,
and the things it buys,
the shiny and new,
the novel -

when the old stuff
is thrown away,
wasted,

and the grandmothers
are stuffed in buildings,
forgotten

by sons
and grandsons
who never visit
when they're sick
and dying.

After all, she's only
the reason they breathe,
to inherit her money,
spend it on big boy toys,

and drown thoughts
of her death
in prime Napa wine.

Down On The Wharf

I see you there
I do
I see you and wonder
how tired a person must be
to sleep sitting upright
on a cold metal bench
as a streetcar rumbles by
as a foghorn blows down on the harbor
as hungry seagulls scream
a few feet away

two days and nights
on a Greyhound
that one time
and I still couldn't
so I wonder...

I'm glad you can
I'm glad you can sleep
and I hope
in a dream
you're flying somewhere
over the ocean
far from here

Dream Catcher

someone gave me
a dream catcher
it's been hanging above my bed
for months now
with its empty net
collecting nothing but dust

I never pay much attention to it
but now I lie here on my back
on a Sunday afternoon
and watch as it slowly twirls
its feathered tassels
swaying in the breeze
from my fan

the room is cool and dark
while outside
the sun bakes
the streets
the rooftops
and every living thing
scurries for shade

I think of nothing
and my eyelids grow heavy
as I watch its gentle movements
its spherical webbed eye
turns this way and that
maybe catching a dream after all

today is today
and tomorrow, tomorrow
for a change
and the brush of feathers
against the air
of a cool dark room
on a scorching summer day
is reason enough to smile

Every Ordinary Day

the driver parked in the alley
and throttled up
the big diesel
to spin the barrel
of the cement mixer faster

and as he sat there
texting his girlfriend
and waiting
for the mixture to be ready
so he could drive
to the site
he had no idea...

that the rattle of his engine
drifted through the open door
of a nearby office
where a man sat
grinding his teeth

a man who
a moment before
had been listening
to the beautiful song
of a bird he'd never heard before

a man whose gut now churned
as he waited
and waited
and resisted the urge
to step outside
and hurl a rock
at the truck's windshield

every ordinary day
is a gauntlet of traps
invisible buttons
and cement trucks
without remedy

Exasperated

I said
"It's meaningless"
and you asked
what I meant by that
so I doubled down with
"what do you mean by 'meaning'?"

you gasped and stuttered
and your face reddened
as you reached
in your pocket
but found nothing

then you turned and ran
up the stairs
and into your room
and I ran too
ran right out the door

because you were either
looking for a gun
or about to jump out the window
like the building
was on fire

and I wasn't sticking around
for either

First Trick

out on a grey straightaway
of the loneliest road
a metal sign points
to where an old mining town
once stood for several years
after a silver strike

the town boasted 26 saloons
the sign says
and brothels too, I imagine
though it doesn't say that

I think about
the working girls
from small towns
back east
hiding here
in tiny rooms
in this sagebrush sea

and I wonder
about their first tricks
how it was for them
when a creature—
a desperate thing
more beast than man—
walked through the door
filthy from the mines
and the lock clicked
as she looked at him
bit her lip
and asked, sweetly,
"wouldn't you like
a bath first, honey?"

Florida Grass

I remember the grass
at my grandma's in Florida
how prickly it was
against my young skin
each green blade
like a tiny
many-edged sword
as I laid on my back
watching thunderstorms gather
and then
at the first heavy drops
running in
to the safety
of her screen porch
to listen
as the thunder crashed
and the rain roared down
onto the metal roof
as though someone
had opened a giant spigot
in the sky

Ghosts Of Flowerpots

the plants
are looking a bit wilted
this morning
and i consider
watering them
first

but time drips
and poetry simmers
like the coffee pot
in the kitchen

so ideas
and writing
must come
before the living
that thirst

as i sit down
and begin typing
i tell myself

i'll do it later

all over the world
we awaken
to our phones
and screens
to horror stories
on the news

and fret about distant others
we cannot help
or twist ourselves
into knots

over politics
and rumors of wars

before noticing
the warm body
in the bed beside us
and is it still breathing

we pour ourselves
into ghosts of flowerpots
while the soil dries
in the next room
and the leaves wilt

our love shrinks
to a harried brush of lips
as we sail out the door

Good Luck With That

to me
bewilderment
is more realistic
than a clear view
of purpose

I shiver
in the presence
of those moon-eyed purveyors
of that particular concept

and flee
to practice
my brand of faith
in dark
secret places

with a flourish
I sweep my hand
across the sky
and insist—

all this
has no need
of your explanations

so go on...
hurl your paper airplanes
toward the living flames

take the Milky Way
by the throat
and squeeze

bash its head in
with your sacred books
and force it to confess

How It Goes

I see her
inside the coffee house
she's looking at me
I can feel it
yet every time I look up
from my screen
her eyes look down at hers

she's good at this game

I get distracted—
social media crap
I tap away
and barely notice
as she walks by

she goes out the door
without a look back
as though she'd never
seen me at all

then, through the window
and through her windshield
across the safety of twenty feet
and two layers of glass
her eyes look directly into mine

two, three seconds pass
then, a smile
and she backs out
and drives off

and what more
can I tell you?

How Lonely We Get

On the sidewalk
a skinny, shirtless man
with matted black hair
dances with a blanket.

He holds it aloft
like a partner
as he shuffles and swings,
then twirls it
over his head,
around his body, criss-cross
like a fighting staff.

He hurls it to the ground,
jumps and stomps on it,
then drags it in circles,
before scooping it up,
draping it over his head
like a monk's robe.

A lover, partner,
enemy and friend,
it shadows him
in stained olive drab
as he roams the city.

Humanity In A Nutshell

The sun is hidden
behind a hill,
and as they walk north
into its light
the boy squeals
"Look Mommy,
I made the sun rise!"

And she laughs
and says,
"You sure did, honey."

I Feel So Cheated

I gotta admit...
It can be disappointing
to discover
that someone isn't quite
the fuck up,
the monster,
the caricature
I needed them to be.

The coworker
who finally
gets his shit together:
starts showing up on time
and doing his job
without spending half the day
playing on his phone
and the other half
hiding in the bathroom.

The politician who,
it is revealed,
does not actually barbecue
and eat poor migrant children
caught at the border,
as the meme had suggested.
(I so wanted to believe it)

Such discoveries rob me
of the joy
of repeatedly bashing them
with my mental bludgeon,
because what is more fun
than that?

I, Grief Counselor

We sat at the bar
sucking back beers
in that smoky roadhouse,
and you went on about it,
and finally said,
"I mean, where is he?
Where did he go?"

Your father, gone,
three months ago
in a freak accident,
his pickup winding up
on its roof in a ditch
for no apparent reason.

You looked at me,
and my lame answer
limped out,
"I believe that
when you're gone,
you're gone."

Spoken like a good
and faithful atheist.
My truth telling
a matter of principle.

You stared at me, nodding
and biting your quivering lip,
Adam's apple working
as you tried swallowing
the bitter fruit of my honesty.

I saw it, and quickly said,
"But what the hell do I know?"

And some years later,
I remember you
angrily saying
that when we die
we just rot in the ground,
and I winced
at how you spit
those words out,
and wished I'd lied
way back then.

I, Misanthrope

With coworkers, roommates,
people at the gym,
the coffee shop...

it usually takes about a year
to begin creeping in, like a stain
spreading under my door.

Then I start to cringe at
seeing their wrinkled morning mugs,
smelling their cheap cologne,
listening to their tireless mouths
farting out the same
stale stories and opinions.

The familiarity
with their catchphrases
and body language
pierces me like a dull blade,
not a comforting nest,
but a steel sprung trap, with jaws
I'd chew my own foot off
to escape.

And they can see it
written in the lines
on my face,
and in the spaces between,
and in black pupils
shaking like balled up
little fists.

I keep silent,
when they ask
"what's wrong?"

Because you can't
tell someone
you wish they were
a pencil sketch
that you could just
scrub off the page.

Although I'm curious
about the facial expression
such an admission
might evoke.

They'd probably laugh.
I must be joking.

Then I'd laugh too.
And let them believe I was.

I Saw That Too

we stood outside the office
waiting
him with head bowed
over smartphone
me craning my head back

he glanced over and saw me
looked quickly
in the direction of my gaze
and seeing nothing
asked what it was

i pointed
"there are buds on that tree"

he looked again
said "oh"
then chuckled
and returned his eyes
to the comforting glow
of the portable hearth
one finger swiping madly
over its fiery glass

a crow glided in
landed on the topmost branch
steadied himself
and folded his wings

a swaying silhouette
against yellow dawn

i saw that too

It Seems So Real

these arguments
seem so real sometimes
like a film
running upstairs
on a continuous loop

I get sucked into them
a pine cone all a-swirl
in a river's eddy
and surprise myself
when I say out loud

"I don't give a shit
what you think!"

sometimes there's people
within earshot

sometimes they look at me
just a glance
because I'm labeled, now
"to avoid"

and that's just fine

I sit and ponder
whether degrees
of schizophrenia exist

clearly it's not as black and white
as people think it is

but then
not much ever is

Journal

I found this journal
among her things
she'd filled the first five pages
with sloppy cursive
written in pain by arthritic hands

I must read slowly
to make out the words
slowly as she walked
during those last days

she misses him
she should've known
should've taken him
to the heart doctor sooner

he was her second husband
and her last
and even after 25 years
she wonders if he loved her
she hopes he did
at least a little

she skipped a few years
and then another entry
still harder to read

she worries
that my mom
will never return
from her trip to China
and about her son
the atheist
will she see him
in heaven?

more years pass
before the last entry
a child's writing
she's 85
can hardly see or walk

if any of us finds this
she wants us to know
God is real
"please believe me"

I'm at the park reading this
I look up
as an old woman with a walker
shuffles along the path

she glances at me
looks away
before I've got a chance
to wave hello

I wanted her to see me wave
to see that I noticed her
I wanted to smile at her
and maybe
have her smile back

Junk Mail

today, as I peeled open
a recalcitrant plastic bag
at the grocery store
I remembered
how you struggled
with the letter opener
then balled your gnarled
arthritic hands into fists
and shook them, gasping
a frustrated little girl again

you threw the envelope down
on the sofa between us
said "Open this for me!"
I tore it open with my finger
looked, and said
"They want to sell you car insurance."
you shook your head
and laughed

you could barely see
anymore

Keep Control

the cashier
at the corner store
has a tattoo on her forearm
that reads—
"Keep Control"
a message that flashes
in and out of sight
strobe-like
as she scrambles
to fulfill the needs
of an interminable line
of smokers
boozers
junk food
and lotto ticket junkies

her eyes dart
jackrabbit wild
and her face
shows the strain
of that "Help Wanted" sign
in the window

I pay for my coffee
with exact change
and she's grateful

I want to tell her
to have a nice day
but she probably doesn't need
the sarcasm
so I say thanks instead

on my way out
I look again at that sign
and just shake my head

King Of The World

Grandpa watches
from the house
across the street
from the park
beer in hand
at nine on a Sunday morning

as the boy
about five
climbs the ladder
of the slide
and proclaims himself
"King of the World"

and down the slide
and on the swing
the merry-go-round
it's "Look, Grandpa!"
"You see me, Grandpa?"

Takes a swig, "Yep."

"Look Grandpa,
there's a million ants!"

"Yep. I see."

after about ten minutes
he calls the boy home
says "we'll come back later"
and they disappear
through the door
as the sun climbs
the blue blue sky
and jungle jim shadows shrink
on the green green grass

Knock On A Distant Door

there's a persistent knock
on a distant door
and you think
you're the only one
who hears it

in time
you learn
that this is not so
but oh the way
the doubtful days
screech by

sometimes you think
you'd gladly trade them
for the saucer-eyed faith
of the herd

but you can't grab on
the propaganda
doesn't stick

the slogans
the symbols
the prescribed paths
don't move you

their battle flags
hang limp and lifeless
even in the wind

if you're lucky
you'll find others
who hear that knock

and build a tribe of them
bonded by an icy faith
that those who huddle
will never understand

Leper

he stands
a good thirty feet
from the door of the coffee shop

he puffs and hacks
spits a glob
of phlegm into a shrub

his face is red
with spots of blue
drawn, lined and drooping

he takes a last deep drag
coughs again
spits

sees me watching
and turns away
shuffles back inside

the day's horrible news
folded under his arm

Like The Red Sea

if I ever wind up
in a bad situation again
on a bad street
with some bad guys
following me
and I just know, man
I know
what's about
to go down

I'm gonna stop walking
and raise the volume
on my internal dialogue
to a shout
complete with lots
of body language—

"What'd you say motherfucker?"
(points at invisible foe
then jumps across sidewalk)

"You heard me, asshole!"
(raises fists, throws punches,
kicks at the air)

and so on

then maybe slap myself
in the face a couple times
roll around on the ground
yelling "get off me, you fuck!"

at the end
of the performance
jump up
and walk right toward them

they'll part
like the Red Sea

Malformed

on the forest floor
there was movement
and when i crouched
to get a closer look
i could see it was a butterfly
struggling to break free

bright yellow and glowing
like a tiny squirming sun
inside the dark shell
of his cocoon

he was halfway out
but seemed stuck
so i pried gently
with my fingertips
until he burst forth

only half formed
with a single brilliant wing
lopsided and flopping in circles
drunkenly on the ground

he would never fly
i couldn't leave him

i awakened with a start
to the crunch
of his tiny exoskeleton
under my boot
feeling sick and hollow
from the dream

light filtered in
through the blinds
i'd slept later than usual

i got dressed
stepped outside
and slowly
raised my eyes to the sky
as though expecting
something to fall

Merge

sometimes you sit inside
on a sunny spring day
and imagine the possibilities
what's out there
all the things you could do
places you could go
people you could meet

hours pass
you crack your knuckles
and wander the house

flip on the tv
nothing
jot some things in a notebook
not much

you look out the window
look in the mirror
check for wrinkles
check for greys
look in the fridge
yep...the expired milk
is still there

and as the sun goes down
you finally step out
to watch
and sigh
as the long shadows
merge

Misophonia

I knew there'd be a name for it,
even before I typed it
into the search engine.

And like every quirk of mine,
it's a symptom of some disorder,
some mental illness.

Because I have them all.
The Internet told me so.
I took all the tests.
OCD? Check, check, check...
Borderline? Check, check, check...
Anxiety, depression,
blah, blah, blah.

This just adds another layer.

I wonder if there's a pill for it...

One that makes my coworker's
atonal humming
sound like a symphony,
the compulsive sniffling
of the man at the coffee shop
sound like wind chimes
in a spring breeze,
and whining dogs
sound like singing songbirds.

While they're at it
they could invent
a pill to make dull people,
dull jobs, a dull life,
seem interesting.

And another to transform
the red faced ravings
of political pundits
into brilliant lectures
by distinguished
and erudite professors.

That would be something
to get hooked on.

People say we take too many pills,
I say give us more!
But give us the right ones.

And I'll be your junkie.
I'll have prescriptions
from different doctors
all over this fucking town!

My Gift To You

to all those
who have crept
into my house
and remained

who have burned
one way or another
and warmed me

know this—
that if I leave suddenly
wind-torn like a page
from your diary
never to return
I carry you

let your tears fall
but not for me

if you need me, talk
I'll listen
best as I can

let the breeze
the ripples
the broken moon
on the pond

all be signs
of my listening

let the silence
in the wake of your asking
be my gift to you

My Old Man's Advice

in Pac Heights
or North Beach
I look around
I admire the architecture
of the gingerbread houses
the doll houses
the churches
and the old apartment buildings

I look at people
at their faces
at their eyes

in the Tenderloin
or downtown
I look ahead
I scan the sidewalk
for needles, bodies,
piles of shit

I look not at
but slightly askew
of the eyes
that my skin tells me
are watching

I puff my chest
swing my arms a little more
I follow my old man's advice
for traversing tough neighborhoods
"Act like you belong there"
It's always served me well

My Optimism

When I remember people,
I can recall every irritating trait,
snide remark, slight,
or petty betrayal.

All of that gets locked
in an inner file cabinet
to be recalled at will,
while any kindness
they may have shown
blows away like a receipt
from the corner liquor store.

In a way it's the opposite
of how I remember
my longest love affair,
with the bottle:
forgetting the shakes, puking,
and shitting my pants,
and the agony
of each morning
before that first gulp
of bedside rotgut,

and remembering the good times,
partying with friends,
wild and uninhibited romps
with strange women met
under dim lights,
the pleasant hazy days
and nights,
when numb time
poured smoothly by
over ice.

And what an odd way
for my optimism
to shine through,
like a sick and jaundiced sun
I must now shield my eyes from.

My Tattoos

you ask
if I have tattoos
and I tell you
I'm covered in them

your eyes
scan my exterior
then blink

you can't see them

what's covered
isn't skin
and these aren't ink

ink only fades
these brighten, darken
or sometimes change color

these are chaos
overwritten
by a half dozen needles
at least

dolphins
over webs
over snakes

over stallions
over masks
over flames

over siamese hearts
wrapped in barbed wire

I'm the only one
who could decipher
the story they tell

and even I just make it up
as I go along

Neighborhood Park

on the evening
of a hundred degree day
the long shadows
creep across the grass
and the people emerge
from air conditioned houses
to walk their dogs
to play ball with their children
to stroll side by side
along the concrete path
losing themselves
in the twilight
joining hands
as the street lamps flicker on
and the night closes in

No One And Everyone Knows

if, on the tail end
of a soar and crash
a week of fever
aching bones
and sleepless nights

if, after you've driven them off
and feel yourself crushed
beneath the knobby sole
of a giant boot
your face in the dirt

and if, as you pound your fist
into the steering wheel
the horn sticks
and you scream
and that scream
somehow becomes laughter
that shakes you to the core
and you can't stop
until it leaves you
on its own

then you're doing just fine
my friend
you've won the day
and it's a victory
like no other
because no one
will ever know
and yet
they all do

Not Cool

on a fine and beautiful morning
I sit at a small table outside the coffee shop
having just read about another mass shooting
here in the land of the free

when a khaki colored Hummer
way too wide for that compact space
backs in anyway
and sits there
idling too long and too loud

finally, the engine's cut
and a man steps out
a stocky man
shorts and T-shirt
civilian clothes
but packing black heat at his right hip

he walks over
metal tables, chairs
bang and screech
as he creates a nest
and I grit my teeth

he comes closer still and leans in
reaches for an electric socket right behind me
his gun barrel an arm's length
from my face

as I scoff and stand up
move to a table far from him
he says "No, man....I'm cool..."

no...
no, you are not cool
fucker
you are so not cool
not on this morning

Not One Of Them

when I think
of all those blurry
desperate nights

the dark rooms
creaky beds
back seats
where we paired

a few of them
with track marks
or questionable
in other ways

my reservations
erased by lust, speed
and whiskey

how close
my flesh
my veins
have likely been
to that bug of all bugs

I thank god
for modern chemistry
for latex
for all those PSAs
that scared the shit
out of we 80's kids
we lazy, apathetic
Gen-X'ers

I never wanted
the plum dark lesions

the protruding rib
and cheekbones

to be a patch
on that ever expanding quilt

but then
neither did they

Ode To A Tired Nurse

she comes in
wearing faded purple scrubs
gets her coffee at the counter
and walks back out again
climbs into a faded blue hatchback
and sits there a moment
she stares unfocused
from dark circles
then grabs the wheel
rests her head on her knuckles
but not too long—
there's no time
to feel sorry for herself this morning
across the street
the hospital windows blaze
as the sun peeks out

One Boxcar After Another

the morning rustles with possibilities
like a plastic shopping bag in the weeds
and i know that today my heart
will surely hop one empty boxcar
after another
and travel landscapes unimaginable
through shadow and light
rocking on the tracks
over mountain trellises
peering pale-knuckled over cliffs
and breathing again
back in the safety of the valley
later to rest
curled up like a worm
in an old sleeping bag
resting on a bed of hollowed grass
beside a river
that lulls it finally
to sleep

On Racism

our parents and grandparents
came north
to Bergen County
to Morris and Sussex
to escape the slums
of Newark and Jersey City
and Paterson
and probably
to get away from "them"

growing up
in suburban New Jersey
in a sea of white faces
it was in the air—
nigger this and spic that

though we didn't really know any
and only saw them
at sporting events
field trips to New York City

I like to think
we spat the epithets
with less venom
than the generation
who taught us

I like to think that

since then
I've known a lot of people
who've tested my childhood faith
helped me scrape off
that old dead skin
and now

I rarely think the words anymore

but racism is tricky
I believe a person
could say racist things
and not be truly racist

I also believe
he could be married to someone
of a different skin tone
and be completely so

this kid I work with
a real history buff
says how ignorant and misguided
people used to be
eugenics and all that bullshit

he says "If I'd lived back then
I'd have—"

"No." I say. "No, you wouldn't have.
Probably not."

One Eyed Sparrow

on the patio
outside the burrito place
I watch the sparrows spar
over crumbs left on the concrete

one hops towards another
charging him
with wings slightly spread
like a puffed up bodybuilder
showing his stuff

the trick works
and the defeated one flies
lands on my table
three feet away

one eye is a black mass of scar tissue
perhaps the claw of an alley cat

he turns to face me with his good eye
reminding me of that homeless guy
down by the river

his left eye was the size of a baseball
purple and swollen shut

at 70 years old
he'd been jumped outside a casino
cold cocked for forty bucks

I had a twenty
so I gave it to him
he cried a little
I put my hand on his shoulder
and squeezed

now the sparrow creeps toward me
then suddenly flies
that scarred eye passes in a blur
inches from my face
and I blink

Ordinary Trauma

I'll take nothing
from those who've been there
in foxholes and firefights
up to their elbows in blood
their ears filled with screams

but after these lives
where we're beaten by bigger, older boys
ridiculed by teachers
shouted at by bosses

after the cacophony of machine shops
and construction sites
the jackhammers
the nail guns
the yellow beasts that strip the soil

even the more serene workplaces
have their bells and buzzers
a million notifications a day
bony little fingers that prod us
toward greater efficiency
as we labor under looming robot shadows
and insomniac camera eyeballs

we are goldfish in a tank
surrounded by mad children
tapping at the glass

back at home
the neighbors slam doors
punch holes in the walls
scream at each other
every Saturday night

a drunk wiggles his key
in the wrong door—
your door—
at three a.m.
then tries to kick it down

lowrider bass thumps
cars backfire
an occasional gun barks
in your neighborhood
everyone holds their breath

a cop lurks in the alley
with a flashlight
"It's ok sir...just looking for a guy..."

you lie awake
sleep through the alarm
arrive late for work
the boss yells, again

daily, we watch
as the earth is raped
by sharp dressed men
with manicured hands
in clean glass towers

as the country's wealth is looted
by those with bloated bellies
their insatiable mouths
still open wide, salivating

are we are supposed
to thicken to all this?

I am peeled thin and raw
as a pink newborn

the dust stings my skin

and at the end of each day
we drink down the gasoline news
chased with whiskey
to stoke our fires

we stash guns
at every door—
one in the car—
and tell ourselves
tell others
"I ain't afraid of shit!"

Origin

first they were outside
the words
the voices
of parents and grandparents
teachers
and counterfeit gods

then came words
from other adults
from songs on the radio
from people on tv

from a barrage of ads
for things i should have
shiny things
that made people smile

and still more
from the mouths of classmates
in the schoolyard
hurled like stones
or sand in the eye

a blitzkrieg of them...
suggesting
advising
commanding
criticizing

i should be this
i should be that

and then one day
somehow
the voices weren't out there

anymore

they were in here
inside
closer than inside

like the ringing
of hammer blows
as a mob of blind sculptors
chiseled a beautiful stone
down to a nub

Owen's Water Chimes

The rain spatters against the window
and I am taken back to his dingy room
in that old flophouse on the north coast,

where we sat 20 years ago
chatting about books and drinking whiskey
during a winter rainstorm,

and he occasionally held up a finger,
interrupting me,
and saying, "Listen!"

He called them his "water chimes,"
the beer cans and bottles
he tossed out the window into the alley,

and heard melodies
in the plinking and plopping sounds
of raindrops on their hollow shells.

I was 25 then, he was 50 years older,
and I thought he was drunk,
or just a crazy old bastard.

Now I sit, listening to the rain,
windblown against the glass
drumming like tiny insistent fingers,

like someone waiting for me
when I'm running late,
but I'm not sure just what for.

Poet, Or Boyfriend

you just want an honest man
you say
one that won't play games
like the others

you don't
trust me on this

as for me
i now realize
i can be a poet
or someone's boyfriend
but not both

i suppose i could
write in secret
use a pseudonym

or else write nothing
but love poems
praising you and us

or about strangers i see
on sidewalks
at the supermarket
imagining their truth
their joys and sorrows

i could write about anything
but my own guts
and marrow
the heart that sometimes feels
like an alien presence
inside me

that tugs me
down strange roads
past signs that read
"do not enter"

all those shocking
and seedy tales
which drew you in
but now...

you're having second thoughts

Police No Come Here

I'm cutting across a corner
of the Tenderloin
on a Saturday morning
and just as I round the corner
onto Van Ness
I hear shouting

a small crowd has gathered
to watch two men shove
then throw punches
in the middle of a narrow side street

as one wrestles the other to the ground
and climbs on top of him
I yell to a security guard
across the street
"You gonna call the cops?"
he looks at me, shrugs

I set my backpack down
and fumble in the pockets
for my phone
but as I begin to dial
I look up
and it's already over

they're on their feet
taunting one another
as they shuffle off
in opposite directions

I walk over to the guard
ask if they'd called 911

he laughs, says

"police no come here
I try before
I wait three hours
they no come
not here
not for homeless person, fighting"

I nod, say
"have a good one"
then head back
toward the hotel

Portrait

It was not you,
but my fanciful brushstrokes
on your blank canvas
that I loved.

An abstract portrait,
beautiful in its impossibility,
loved even more
because of it.

But it was stripped from me
by shifting winds,
like a kite
that flew too high
and snapped its string.

It could not
endure the storms,
and crashed to earth
tattered and broken.

I knelt beside it,
gingerly touching
its torn edges,
brimming eyes gazing
at its still vivid colors,
wondering
if it could be
salvaged or sewn,

as you slipped
quietly out the door.

Psychologists

literally
those who study the soul
but make no mistake
it's a dirty swamp
not a sterile, pristine laboratory
and no one ventures in
who isn't broken
drawn to fog and darkness

it's a place to hide
like the church used to be
a place to put themselves
back together
or at least
seal some of the cracks

and maybe
they fix it
part of it
and crawl out again
all duct tape
and bailing wire
under business casual

it's not exactly
the blind leading the blind
but they're squinting
through the grey
same as you
believe me

and they don't know
where the snakes are
any better
than you do

Red Shoe

at the park
a single red shoe
lays on its side
in a grassy field

I wonder
how they can forget
such a bright
and beautiful thing
such a necessary thing
and won't they miss it?

I leave the park
I leave the shoe behind
in case someone
comes looking

as I walk the neighborhood
everyone I see
is missing a shoe
they limp or hop along
down the sidewalks
nod to one another
and wave hello
as though this is normal

when I arrive home
I notice
one of my sandals
has fallen off
somewhere
but I don't know how
or when that happened
or where to look for it

and suddenly that red shoe
glaring like a bloodshot eye
from the middle of that green field
doesn't seem so absurd

Renofornia

I see them at the corner store,
sleepy eyed Mexican men
caked in grey mud
and carrying hard hats,
fueling up on caffeine and sugar
at 7 a.m. on a Saturday,

so they can climb
three stories of scaffolding
and work all day
with trowels in hand,
finishing the exterior walls
of the new apartment building
next door.

Apartments they won't be able
to afford.

Apartments to house
more Bay Area refugees,
people who will see
1500 a month
for a one bedroom
as a bargain,
until they get a load
of the wages here
east of the mountains.

And soon it'll be
just like San Francisco,
where I once spent a pleasant
and sweaty evening
with a Salvadorian woman
in a studio apartment
divided between her

132

and a roommate by bedsheets
nailed to the ceiling.

Talk about walls
being paper thin.

Robbed

his name was Rob
"like, to steal"
as he used to joke
and he gave me
my first ever snort
and taste of the crystal
in his single wide
up in Sun Valley
"Felony Flats"
or "Scum Valley"
as we locals call it

it didn't feel
like anything
had been stolen
more as if he'd handed me a key
to unlock a door
I'd never known
could be opened

as we drove
to the store
for more beer
I swore I could move
the stars
the city lights
like chess pieces

where had this ability
been hiding?

some time later
after three days
and nights
of nonstop partying

I saw my face
in the mirror
after a dark
and dehydrated piss

there was definitely
something missing
besides about ten pounds of meat
from my bones

but from the living room
my new friends
called to me
that the pipe
was filled
and was I gonna hit this shit
or not?

I turned
from my reflection
and went out
with a clenched smile
heart racing
fingertips eager to burn
on the blackened
hot glass

Rusted Glamour

the journey through hell
becomes glamorous
on the page
until the ink
begins to burn

it's like reading
about the rebel
the anti hero
about Holden's life
or old J.D. himself

the hermit
for whom human faces
human souls
were withered flowers
rotten fruit

but live your own life
like that
and the glamour
quickly rusts

I met a homeless guy
down by the river
with a copy of Catcher
in an old backpack
we chatted awhile...

I'll bet every hobo in America
owns a copy
creased and folded
fat with dogeared pages
greasy with the despair
of the seeker

San Francisco Girl

she sails through
the just-turned-red light
cranking the pedals
blonde hair sideways

a horn blares
she flips the bird
then smiles

her heart shaped sunglasses
flash in the light
like a kiss blown
my way

I hold my breath
as I watch her go
down the hill
and out of sight

my skin all goosebumps
in the afternoon sun

Sapling

on a small, curbed-in island
a sapling sprouts
from an old stump

it taps into thick roots
that buckle the earth
and heave it toward the sky

roots that split concrete
and shatter blacktop
like a nest of subterranean snakes

and I wonder
if they'll leave it alone
to drink sunlight and reach higher

or if its long morning shadow
will be as tall
as it ever grows

Say It!

if they could just
help themselves
all those evil, hateful
vindictive people
all those angry people

if they could just
help themselves
and stop being that way
and be more like us
just be happy
you know?

we choose our happiness
we could be that way
if we wanted
angry and hateful

but no
we choose this way
we choose to smile
we choose to love others

it's a choice
isn't it?
well?

say it's a choice.
say it!
speak up
goddamn you!

Scavenger

the truck clatters
down the quiet alleyway
its bed overflowing
with wire, pipe
an old TV
a bookcase

it screeches to a halt
beside a green dumpster
and a tall, lean man
climbs out
rummages a bit
pulls out an old wooden box

he inspects it
then tosses it in
sees me looking
and gives a little salute-wave

then he jumps in
slams the door
and heads on to the next
as the sun climbs
to fill the potholed alley
with a brilliant light
and the blacktop glitters
like crushed diamonds

Sing Emptiness For Me

Though we're just friends
—mostly online—
and have never been more,
I think what put me here
was seeing you, yesterday,
beautiful and dark haired,
but attached, and
traveling the world
with your man—
India, England,
Ireland, next on the list.

You asked how I'd been,
if I had a girlfriend
and why not, as i squirmed,
and mumbled, while staring
at the dirt on your shoes,
stumbling through ad-libbed lines
that explained nothing.

If I could paint,
or sculpt, or sing,
maybe then I could
paint, sculpt, or sing
emptiness...express it
in some way better
than these dark squiggles,
looking this morning
like desiccated earthworms,
sunbaked and dead
on a concrete slab.

Or I could stare at the blank page
and sit in silence, write nothing.
Let the mourning dove cooing outside
under last night's lingering rain clouds
express it for me.

Snipe Hunt

as you hunted them
and they ran for cover
someone shouted "Why?"

you answered for all the shooters
when you said
"Because I'm angry!"

then you squeezed the trigger again
drowning them out
drowning you out
drowning it out

a snipe hunt
if ever there was one
you killed that day
but missed your target

you—all of you—
could burn the world
into a flaming marshmallow on a stick
and never kill that bastard

it hides
where you don't dare peek
closer than beneath your pillow
your fingertips
or the backs of your eyeballs

So, What Do You Do?

He asked what I do and I said,
"Well, I usually wake up early and piss first,
then brush my teeth if it's a weekday,
or if it's a weekend I'll skip it
and head straight for the coffee pot,
then to the computer to get a little writing done..."

I enjoyed the way he smiled at me,
like you do at a crazy,
cracked out street person
who's telling you their story,
and you really want outta there,
but there's no way out.

Ok, I've never actually done this.

But I think we all should...
just to throw off
the natural order of the universe,
and this not so subtle way
of determining my social caste
and whether or not
I'm worthy of your time.

Fuck you.
That's what I do for a living.

Spill It

better still
than the bullet
the noose
the bottle of pills
write...just write

fuck Hank's advice
and fill the world
with lousy writing

tell, if you must
tell us everything
and show nothing
I'd rather be told the truth
than shown a lie

spill your venom
your tears
across cyberspace

fuck what all those role models
and father figures told you
about being a man
they all lied
just like TV
the movies
and religion

so spill it all
shout it
in stuttered
and broken sentences
from the rooftops

let your hollowpoint words
whistle past our ears

but don't place your screams
in our mouths
in our children's mouths
anymore

Spit Him Out

I suspect I'll bump into you someday
at the grocery store
or wherever
and be asked to explain
why I blew off your wedding
and why I unfriended you

but when we reunited
years after high school
and I met the new you—
tattooed, loud
rabid right wing
gun totin' redneck
("Obama would look good
between my crosshairs!")

then, I met
your online doppelgänger
and saw what an ugly
son of a bitch he is...

I remember
the awkward kid
the shy one
the outsider
like me

now, like a method actor
you've lost yourself
in your character

he's chewed you up
but won't spit you out

Taking My Medicine

I was cleaning up the joint
after closing
and as I mopped
what seemed like acres of floor
in the empty building
it just got louder

I thought they'd all gone
but they weren't gone
there was a whole chorus
the voices just came faster
a whirlwind of them
recriminations like hailstones
pelted me from inside

I trembled as I worked
tried to shake them
determined not to miss
a square inch of floor
but I was waiting
for the world to shatter
even hoping for it

that's how I always thought
It would be
like staring at a giant tv screen
that suddenly loses reception
the picture turns to snow
and then collapses
to a pinpoint
a blank screen
and silence
blessed silence

but that never happened
it just got louder
faster

I finished mopping
locked up
then drove to the hospital
the mental hospital
where they checked me out
after I waited for two hours
but then said
they couldn't prescribe anything
unless I checked myself in

I looked at the door
with its little window
of thick, unbreakable glass that led
"back there"
down a long hallway
where I'd be among "them"
eating, sleeping
walking among "them"

I looked at that
and said no, and left
I sat in my car
in the parking lot
and screamed
then drove to the liquor store
and home
where I drank my medicine down

That's About It

one pill worked
for awhile
until I became mean
as a snake again
and hissed at anyone
who got close

the doc gave me
a higher dose
then...
a second pill

I saw where
this was headed

so I hit the booze again
poured that
over the whole cocktail
and blew it all to shit

locked myself in a room
for three months
with a bottle of vodka

now I'm a teetotaler
"In recovery"
sort of...

the pills are flushed
but I take my vitamins

and even try on a mask
of spirituality
now and again

too much trouble—
it keeps falling off
when I yell at people
in traffic

or when I bury my face
in a pillow
to scream at the world

I work
I write
and I rage

there's not much love
but sometimes I smile
sometimes I even laugh

that's about it

The Autodidact

to be sure
there are gaps
in my education
I have read many books
and some would say—
the wrong ones

but now these gaps
seem like a blessing
like driving through the redwoods
early in the morning
as the low hanging sun
flashes strobe-like
through the interstices
of those massive trunks

instants of illumination
that blind or enlighten
and sometimes both
but each one
a mystery that re-enchants
the too-known world
and baffles me
in a wonderful new way

The Awful, Petty Truth

I swear
being asked
about your day
can be
one of the most excruciating things
there is

I wonder
how many wife murders
have been committed
simply because of it

but after the neighbors call
and the cops arrive
to find a man sitting on the couch
baseball bat caked with blood and hair
by his side
he says

"it was another guy"
because you can't admit
to the awful
petty
truth

The Bathroom Situation

San Francisco
is never NOT a maze
of scaffolding
orange barricades
and construction fences

cranes plentiful as skyscrapers
dot the skyline
and jackhammers
ring through the streets

and because of all this
you can find a port-a-potty
almost anywhere
which is great
except they're locked

I understand why though
because of that time I—
my bladder fit to burst—
finally found
a public bathroom kiosk
but when I got to the door
three women sat inside
passing a glass pipe

I stood there
until one saw me
smiled a mostly toothless smile
and offered to blow me
for twenty bucks

I had the twenty
but I declined
went somewhere

and bought a sandwich instead
used the bathroom
at the restaurant
"for paying customers only"

The Empty Plate

Some still cling to
sagging branches,
defiantly green,
their edges frost tinged
in November's chill,

while others
are faded yellow,
or shockingly red,
dark as plums, nearly black,
or bright orange, browning
to crisp flakes fluttering,
crunching underfoot,

scattered shreds of decay
filling sidewalk cracks,
becoming dust carried high,
traveling the winds, and later,
floating in shafts of early sunlight,
settling soundlessly
on the ground,

and being tilled
by a rusty shovel
into the thawing spring soil
of a widow's vegetable garden,
black under fingernails,
bright green, yellow or red again
upon a lonely dinner table,

chewed slowly, savored
under the watchful eyes
of a framed photo
sitting across from her,
beside an empty plate.

The End Of The Story

two women and I
converged on a gravel path
and as we approached
without acknowledgment
I heard one's voice as it swelled
and she told her friend—

"....I guess I did it
because I was sick of being alone
and lonely but then..."

her voice faded
and was swallowed up
by distance
and the crunch of sharp stones
beneath our collective feet

but I already knew
the end of the story

The Home Of The Wind

the want to comes
from the same place
as the wind
and it goes back there
just as easily

if you could find it
you could ask why
my love was so short
and why I still
tear at myself
for what was never mine

but don't ask me
where it is
or how to get there

I only know
its breezes
its gusts and gales
as they blow
from one direction
or another

as they push me
towards or away
and then halfway back
towards traces of you

The House Where I Live

as I drive east on I-80
following the river out of town
the thought seizes me
as it sometimes does—

I could keep going
this road goes home—
I mean HOME-home
and beyond

all the way to the GWB
the Atlantic
it'd be four days of driving
but I could do it

fuck tomorrow morning
and fuck the job
just go

then I remember
HOME-home
ain't been home
for years

I turn off the highway
I park the car
and stare at the river for awhile

I lose myself
in the patterns of ripples
on the water's surface

then I sigh
climb back in the car
and drive back to town
back to the house
where I live

The Impossible Stage Of You

for each of us
there is one
who becomes background
and stage
for all those who follow

and as they step out
they have no idea—

how harsh the glare
of the spotlight

where the loose boards are
the protruding nails

how unforgiving
the audience

and the critics
in the balcony
scribbling notes

perched vulture-like
on the edge of their seats
as they anticipate
a slip
or fall

The Legend Of Butt-Fuck Nowhere, U.S.A.

In the middle of an alkali flat
with clumps of dry grass
jutting like tufts of hair
from the poorly shaven head
of a mad hermit,
sits a travel trailer,
surrounded by barbed wire.

I think about it, sometimes...
buying a little patch
of sand and sagebrush
miles from the nearest town,
parking a trailer on it,
and just living there like that...

The coyotes will learn to trust me.
I'll join in their hunt,
yipping and howling along.

Crows will soar to my calls
and perch on my outstretched arm,
as I stroke their feathers.

I'll spend days
sitting on my roof,
burning myself in the sun
and singing songs
in an invented language
understood only by me
and the sky,
and by night I'll dance
around bonfires,
naked as a tribesman.

My nearest neighbors
will peer at me
through binoculars, whispering,
"What the hell's he doin' now?"

I'll fire a shotgun in the air
whenever someone comes near,
and legend will grow
at the local watering hole.

"I hear he's a child molestor."
"Escaped from a looney bin."
"Wealthy stockbroker, lost it all."
"He's an alien, I'm tellin' ya'll..."
"Shut the fuck up, Al!"
"Hahaha!"

On trips to town
I'll speak to no one,
pretending to be
deaf and dumb.

And when I die,
my coyote and crow
brothers and sisters
will fill their bellies
with my stringy and aged meat,
dragging my carcass into the desert
and devouring me so thoroughly,
I will seem to have disappeared.

Then curious throngs
will flock to my doorstep,
rummage through my things,
and wonder...

"Maybe the girl's father killed him."
"Hauled back to the nuthouse."
"Probably went back to Wall Street."
"The mother ship came and got him...
didn't ya'll see that light the other night?"
"Al, I'm tellin' ya..."

The Lie Everyone Tells

I knew it
since I was a boy,
listening to the grownups talk,
when the question was asked.

Because I saw their faces
through the windows
of Mom's car,
as they drove
to and from their jobs,
sucking on cigarettes,
drinking coffee,
usually never meeting
my child's eyes,
though I knew
they knew
I was watching.

And I saw
the faces
of the checkers
at the supermarket,
and the people
who worked at the shoe store,
or at the doctors office,
or anywhere else
and the expressions they wore.

And how Dad
came home from work
every evening,
dragging a bit
through the front door,
followed by a draft
of cold winter air

and silence.

And how the teachers at school
acted every morning,
and how harshly
they often treated us,
always,
"For our own good."

But when people were asked,
they always told you.

I said it too,
over the weekend
at a barbecue
with friends I hadn't seen
in awhile.

"So, what are you doing now?
Do you like it?"

The Night At My Throat

I did this to myself
with that three-hour nap
this afternoon
and now the night
is at my throat

go...go somewhere
drive out into the desert
to a blacker sky
where the stars
seem too bright

or head downtown
roam the streets
because out there
swathed in neon
is something better
than here

meanwhile I pace
the quiet of the house
as it gnaws at me
like rats chewing
at the walls

I step outside
and gaze
at a few
dim
stars

The Old Crone Does Hard Time

I generally cringe
when I hear glassy eyed, new age types
talking about transmigration of the soul
as though it were an absolute fact, like gravity.

But there's something to this idea
of the "Old Soul."

Because there's an old woman
in here. A real old crone. Nasty as fuck.
She's been around, ya know?
Been through some shit.
Jumped from one skin sack
to another, for who knows how long.

She knows all the tricks.
The mercenary ways
of brain and heart.
She's heard every bullshit excuse,
and alternately cackles
or groans at most
of what people say and do.

She sits on the front porch
of my house human,
slowly rocking in her chair,
spittoon on one side,
shotgun on the other.
Loaded and cocked.

I can picture her standing
before a tribunal of the powers that be,
before being sent back here
from the underworld.

I see a half-circle of black hooded men,
their faces lost in shadow,
as she practically begs
"Please guys, not another body..."

But they laugh,
and off she goes,
flipping the bird on the fly,
and her "fuck you" translates
into my first ever scream,
as I am yanked out
into the cold.

The unsuspecting parents
wind up with a baby
who looks at grownups like idiots
when they babble at him
or play peekaboo.

People say he seems pissed off.
Resentful. (Well, no shit!)
He doesn't smile much,
or pose for photos,
or play well with other children.

And doesn't cry
when the goldfish,
or the dog,
or people,
die.

He knows better.
Or she does.

The Poet In The Family

Though my mother
read a lot more books
and wrote a lot more
I think it was really my father
who was the family poet

like when teenage Brian
would head out
on a Friday night
and he'd say with a grin
"Make sure you sheathe ol' one eye!"

or when he had a bad case
and shifted uncomfortably on the couch
growling about what he called
"inflammation of the blowhole"

or deep in January
when he'd come in the back door
followed by a blast of arctic air
and say "Goddamn!
It could freeze the balls
off a brass monkey out there!"

The Pulse

other cities
always seem more interesting
but it's good, once in awhile
to prowl the streets of your own
to feel it's pulse in your toes

today, as I drive towards downtown
streets are barricaded everywhere
and I backtrack two, three times
finally find street parking, unmetered
(I'm a fucking local....I ain't paying!)

I park
start walking
past the bus station
the street people
with shopping carts
or duffel bags

past a casino
where a guy shoves chips
in my face
like a dope dealer
offering a little taste

past the courthouse
I helped build, years ago
with its strange sculpture—
a flat piece of steel
drilled with large holes—
and wonder
if this was the artist's idea
of a joke—

a rusty, Swiss cheese abomination
in front of a place
that dispenses justice

I walk on
across the Virginia Street bridge
find the source
of all those barricades—

the beer-fest
of course
white tents
line the main drag
iced down kegs
and frosty glasses
people drinking
smiling, laughing
fuck!

I'm thirsty
and painfully sober

I should leave
maybe head down East 4th
where the hookers stroll
but no...
too early in the day
they're shut up
in cheap rooms
with the shades pulled tight
sleeping off last night's horror show
of hideous bodies
souls, and cock

I walk back
to where the river flows
green and swollen
head west
toward the mountains

cottonwood seed
fills the air
tiny puffs
of a million daydreams
float, rise and fall
in the brilliant June sunshine

The Shadow Of A Mountain

the morning sun peeks
over a mountain
about a hand's width
taller than the horizon

the true horizon
if I could see
through the earth

which means the sunrise
actually happened
a half hour ago

and isn't everything
like this?

everything we see
everything that shocks, delights
or surprises
happens before we see it

behind the shadow
of a mountain

The Shut-In

my friend warns me
how looney she is
never goes out
just stays locked up
in the house
with her dozen cats

I drive over there
get to the door
and ring the bell

she opens it halfway
stands in the space
blocking my view inside

her long grey hair is matted
she wears a stained green bathrobe
and holds a cat under each arm

In one hand is a twenty
I take it, then ask
if she wants me
to bring the pizza inside

"No!" she says
and opens her hand
the cat under that particular arm
is a mangy calico
he stares through me
with bright yellow eyes

I put the box in her hand
she grabs it
says "keep the change!"
then slams the door

she seems ok to me
she creeps me out less
than that Mormon family
with the dozen kids
and the wife
with the long pleated skirt
and the too-wide smile
who always insists
that I come in

The Squatter

I don't know
why you stay, love

why here, in this hovel
as the eviction notices
rustle outside the door

why, as the floor rots
and the walls creak

or how you flourish
with the windows
boarded up

how you still reach
toward a sliver of light
a crack in the ceiling

where the sparrows
squeeze through
build their nests in the rafters

their tweets and chirps
would drive anyone mad
and yet

you smile, love
like a prickly flower
in the dark

The Surface Alone

the shoes
wouldn't tell you much
maybe they're too tight
they squeak

or they're old
they stink
they've got holes
the pavement burns
a stone gets in there
rattles around
and bruises your heel

but to explore
another's head
and heart—
their soul, if you prefer

an ocean
that even on the surface
is so vast...

every ripple, wave, and eddy
a cause
an effect
an infinite web
a pattern
a secret code
no god could decipher

not to speak
of the depths

swim in that
for a mile
for a few feet—

you can't even
dip your toe

The "Typical" American Male

Bullied into a Hollywood stereotype
of masculinity, our young,
soft clay brains
imprinted with action heroes,
western stars with blazing guns
and porno studs with huge cocks.

We must win the bar brawl,
bare fisted, five on one,
single handedly
tame the lawless town,
fuck every woman
without being swamped
by tangles of emotion.

Never apologize,
show remorse,
confusion,
or weakness.

Be the strutting,
crowing rooster,
high upon a fence post,
creation trembling
in his presence.

Not a mid 30s
pizza delivery guy,
drinking himself stupid
in a studio apartment every night,
jerking off to porn
until he's rubbed raw.

Then stalking the one woman
who ever loved him
on social media at 3 a.m.,
a virtual prowler
and rapist.

Or venting bilious
clouds on Internet forums,
spewing comments
on news articles
with sarcasm sharp
as a samurai sword,
hatred finely tuned
as a baby grand.

Nigger and faggot and cunt
rolling off his fingertips
as he plays those keys,
feeding on their angry responses,
cackling drunkenly until sunrise.

The View From The Arena

go on...
give them some of that good advice
now that you're drowning in it yourself
show them how gracefully
you thrash to the other side
when the only thing
that keeps you
grabbing handfuls of water
is rage

give them your words of wisdom now
smart guy
"relax...go easy on yourself"
all that stuff
tell them to talk to someone
shout it at them
through your locked door

tell them to focus on something
outside the noise and the swirl
a face in the crowd
a flower
a car horn
when all you hear
is the static
of a long highway
between radio stations

show them how to
"just breathe"
like you do
with your head
in the lion's mouth

Their Way

whatever else
let me die
with the sun
on my face

when I think of you
in that white room
under the glare and buzz
of those lights

just waiting, now
after the stroke
the feeding tube
resuscitation
refused

I wish I'd picked up
what was left of you
carried you out
and laid you
on the grass
to wither quickly
as a leaf

but we are civilized
we don't do things
like that

they'd have tackled me
handcuffed me
if I'd tried

laid your body back
in that shivering room

to die
their way

There Was No Need

he'd grown
into a bitter old bastard
so i threw a bit of meanness
back at him
and he winced, said
"didn't anyone ever teach you
to respect your elders boy?"

i reminded him
"this is America...
we don't give a shit
about our elders here."

i could've reminded him
how he warehoused
his own mother
in a sterile white place
never visited her
and then stuck her
unceremoniously
in the family plot
with the rest
of their orphaned bones

but from the look
on his face
i could see
there was no need

This Branch

you wouldn't ask a bird
why this branch
and not that one

why then
do you ask me
where I come from
and where I go?

you could point out
to the bird
how thick and sturdy
that branch is
compared to the flimsy thing
he clutches
that shakes with every breeze

but if the bird
could speak
he would tell you—

I flew here
landed here
because
it is THIS branch

This Is Not About A Dog

I'm not really a dog person,
and yet I own one,
but maybe "own" isn't quite right...

He drags me through each day,
tugging and sometimes chewing
on the leash, growling and snapping
at smiling strangers and rustling bushes,
sniffing at crotches, assholes,
and congealed sidewalk stains.

He yanks me forward
into groaning dark corners
or back down rusted alleys
littered with faded empty cans
and shards of broken glass
glittering enticingly.

Sometimes I'd like
to just turn him loose,
let him piss and shit
in all their front yards
and precious flower beds,
and bite every hand
that dares to pet him.

But they'd probably sue,
because he's "mine".

I grow tired of walking him-
or him walking me-
so I lock him up
in his dog pen for awhile,
but then he just paces,
whining and barking

and driving me nuts,
so off we go again.

And when evening comes
and my feet are dragging
and I could not dig up a smile
with a backhoe,
someone will ask
what's wrong.

Usually I ignore them,
but sometimes I'm compelled
to explain about
my incorrigible mutt.

When I'm finished
they usually look around,
eyes puzzled and searching,
then back at me,
and blink.

Except a few,
who hang their heads,
and close their eyes,
nodding sadly.

This Is Not A Pen

this is not a pen
in my hand
but a chisel

and every mark
on the page
is a hammer blow

as I chip away
at these walls
made of old bones

that crumble
one grey splinter
at a time

Tiny Tyrant

a large black fly
lands beside me
as I sit on a park bench

he inches closer
stops and rubs his forelegs together
like an aspiring tyrant

like a tiny man eager
to get his hands
on this new territory

to build a buzzing empire
in the rot
of its imminent demise

I whisk him away
close my eyes
and lift my face

the sun shines
faded red
through my eyelids

Togetherness

In an alley
two women sit
side by side,
backs against bricks.

They sit
shoulder to shoulder,
not noticing me
as I walk by.

Their heads
are bowed in silence,
eyes fixed on spikes
stuck in pale arms,
elbow crooks purpled.

Bodies slump,
lean into one other
as orange plungers
are pressed.

To My Younger Version

you'll find fragments
of my sermon
beneath a hundred mattresses
and written on the walls
of a thousand dive bars

you'll find my words
on the lips
of friends, enemies
lovers and haters
of brutal bosses
junkies, thieves
and the inexplicably saintly
placed in your path

you'll collect scraps
of it from dozens of towns
across the country
for twenty
twenty five years

and throw them
in a shoebox
to look at
when you're tired
and broken
rub your chin
and ponder

If I'd read it aloud to you
in its entirety
when you were 18, 21, or 25—

I know damn well
what you'd have done

so this is how I'll do it
you thick headed
young man, you
because I know
this is the only way

To No One In Particular

We chatted for hours,
fingers tapping
frantic messages,
lots of smiles, winks,
and LOLs,
you being a bit quicker
on the draw
than I.

I wished I could
hear your voice
on the telephone.
Maybe I'd ask,
but later...
don't want to spook you,
seem like a creep.

After saying goodnight,
I showered,
all tingly as I
lathered my hair
and imagined
our life together-
two quirky loner types,
half insane poets
just jagged enough
to fit each other's
broken edges.

The shampoo ran
into my eye,
and I blinked,
rinsed it away, cursing
and snapping out
of the dream
I hung on pixels
on a screen.

Too Damn Fast

be grateful, also
for the hours spent trapped
in unwanted conversation

for traffic jams
and sleepless nights
in twisted sheets

for long lines
and the chatty cashiers
at their bottlenecks

for the chalkboard nails
on the clock hands
that drag and screech

and the goosebumps
the headaches
and the grinding teeth

you're always saying
how fast it all goes
too damn fast

Too Sensitive

been told this
since early on
and reminded of it
all along the way

and it's a bad thing
for a smaller than average boy
on the playground
or a long haired teenager
on the construction site

a thin skinned young man
shacked up with a whore

but now it has become
one of many things
about which
a fuck
can no longer be given

I picture it
this thing inside me
black and scarred
like my liver
on the outside
still soft and pink within

and I'll mine
every ounce of flesh
from this bastard
and feed it
to the world
before I'm dust

Tough Decisions

several months
before I was conceived
in springtime, 1973
the high court decided—

the sewing needles
the toxic potions
the back alley clinics
no longer necessary

and as I grew inside
I might've heard
whispers of watergate
crime waves
the embargo
the stock market crash
and runaway inflation

it must have seemed
to those two youngsters
like the good old days
of the 50s world
they'd known
were over

"What the hell is going on?"

and as I felt the surge
of adrenaline
felt her heart beat faster
every evening at six
when I heard
the familiar drone
of the newsman's voice
from inside that tiny ocean

I might've wondered
if I'd make it

It's been 46 years
and as I listen
to the news now
in 2019

I still wonder
about that

Two Impossible Years

we drank and snorted
loved and laughed
and clawed at each other
through two impossible years

and once had makeup sex
in the bathroom stall
of our favorite dive bar
as our feet slid on slivers
of broken beer bottles

if I'd known then
that those years
would never come again
and how short
they'd seem now...

I'd still have pissed it away
I'd have drank more
I'd have fucked you harder
so everyone at the bar
could hear us

we'd have gotten applause
when we walked out
instead of just a sly grin
from old greybeard
sitting on his corner stool

Vampires

They shove cameras
in their faces
and ask the question—

of the bloodied and defeated
of jilted husbands and wives
of the mothers of stillborns

of the poor bastards
whose livelihoods
have just been eliminated
due to "restructuring"
or technology

of junkies
remembering their former
youthful promise

of men on their way
to prison
or the electric chair

the unblinking
cyclopean lens trained
on their eyes
to detect the slightest twitch
or tremor in those pools
between the words
and the truth

"how do you feel right now?"

Virtual Reality

the young guys
in the warehouse
are talking
virtual reality
and how cool
this game is
and what about that one?

and I think
"Fuck!"

my whole life
it's as though
I've had a chip
embedded in my brain
a program
a simulation
that provides me
with an enhanced
but false picture
of the world
alternately brilliant
or black

and it's been
my life's work
to dig
that
sucker
OUT!

and you bozos
wanna go through life
with a helmet
glued to your head

maybe...
I'm a relic
maybe the passion
for truth
has become as quaint
in this bold new era
as tearing oneself
to shreds
over lost loves

they oughta lock me up
in a museum somewhere

charge 20 bucks a pop
to watch the madman
claw at the reality
of the glass
between us

We Tried

for many of us
booze was a tool
a monkey wrench
that loosened our bolts
and let us rattle a bit

it was anger management
a friendly face
a kind word and a smile
an attempt at compassion
or love

we could file down
our sharp edges
and blend in
without cutting you

eventually
the tool fatigued
and shattered

it didn't work anymore
but at least we tried

you're welcome
fuckers

What I Learned In Group Therapy

We sat in a semicircle
as the therapist talked about
"radical acceptance":
a technique to allow
our rebellious minds
to better accept reality.
You know... reality:
traffic jams,
tyrannical bosses,
people that cut in line...

things like that.

To absorb these unpleasantries
in a more dignified manner
than screaming "Fuuuuck!"
and driving down the shoulder,
walking off the job
and getting drunk for a week,
shoving the asshole
into the candy rack...

to kinda curb
these sorts of reactions.

She must have been
about 27-28, a brunette
with a pretty face
and pale skin.
I watched her mouth
as she talked,
her red lipstick faded
at the end of the day.

As she turned

to write something
on the blackboard
my eyes switched
to the twin globes
of her round ass
cradled in a tight black skirt.

When she'd finished talking
I raised my hand, said,
"I'm not clear on how
we're supposed to do this, exactly."

She smiled at me
like a stupid child,
and standing there
with all her framed diplomas
flashing in the background,
gave a convoluted answer
which amounted to,
"You just do it."

An ad slogan,
from a twenty something
six figure expert.

What Kind Of Soul Today

on good days
it's slippery
their barbs
their sneers and scowls
even their laughter
slides off
like a fried egg
off a well greased pan

usually it's a ditch
overgrown with brambles
far flung seeds that flew here
to rot among the impaled trash
that rustles on the thorns
and the throats
of empty bottles that howl
in the seeking wind

when it rains
the culvert chokes
and can't swallow it all
the water rises and overflows
out into the street
filling dirty puddles
that reflect a grey dawn

What's Most You

sometimes I'm asked
why this
or why that

why do you arrive so early?
why don't you talk to me anymore?
why do you sit over there
and eat lunch under that tree
instead of with us?

I usually don't answer
just look at them
in silence

there might be a why
there might be one
or more than one
but they're mine
not yours

sometimes these whys
are all you've got
they are more you
than you could ever be

Working Class Vacation Strategies

I eat a lot
of peanut butter sandwiches
on road trips these days

it's what a working guy does
if he wants to take a trip
to San Francisco or Monterey
without going into debt
and still have a bed
to sleep in

but those motels
ain't getting any cheaper
pretty soon
I'll curl up in the back seat
lie half awake all night
as I await the tap-tap-tap
of a cop's flashlight on the window
"Can't park here!"

I'll sigh and move on
drive the city streets
or up and down Pacific Coast Highway
in the darkness
looking for another spot

and instead of peanut butter sandwiches
I'll just fast for two or three days
pretend I'm a Native American
on a vision quest
maybe I'll glimpse the future...

never mind
I already have
it ain't good

You Are Still Beautiful

the midsummer sun
is too much
for them now

they whiten and shrivel
bloodless as a matriarch
in her casket

but with edges
dipped in red
like too bright lipstick
hastily brushed

I pluck the petals
from a blossom
crumple them to powder
sift them fine as dust
between my fingers

and as they float
and drift to the ground
I assure them
of their indestructible beauty

You Can Only Fall For A Stranger

We are so lonely,
we fall for strangers' masks
on our computer screens,
and their words
of shared pain
and understanding,
new faces and stories
like hooks to hang
our tattered hopes on.

Or meet people at bars
and shack up
after a drunken one nighter,
try to make it work
through the yelling, distrust,
and incompatibility.

After they're gone
we roam empty houses,
grasping at gods,
whispering prayers
and questions at three a.m.,
and then, hearing nothing,
go fix a drink,
and then another.

Eventually, we drag ourselves
out of some gutter
we've wallowed in
for long enough,
and reinvent,
like the celebrities do,
and then fall deeply
for this self we imagine,
brightly painted,

fierce and unafraid,
reborn.

Unlike those earlier drafts,
stained and torn,
wadded up
and buried in the trash.

You Only Think So

not that anyone asks
but if they did
often, you couldn't say
what's wrong anyway

and not because it's too big, no...
it's easy to say—
a friend died
my girl dumped me
I got fired

but because the thing
is so petty
so small—
a glance
a vibe
a habit

someone laughs
in your naked moment

a splinter of glass burrows
stabs deep
and unexpected

you squirm
against this tiny seed
spilling its darkness
testing your faith
that you are human

R. Keith is the author of eighteen books including Wild Rose Country (Cajun Mutt Press), FLOP (Rust Belt Press), A polemic study of negative space (mu press) and Plungent, the

(Alien Buddah Press)

"What is a book? It is just a fable with faces! Novels are rubbish, too, written as rubbish, merely for idle people to read..."

-from Poor Folk, Dostoyevsky

Alien Buddha Press 2019

STUMPS
short stories from r. keith

ISBN: 9781686413872

Alien Buddha Press 2019

David Boski has somehow acquired the spiritual pens of Dan Fante, Wantling, Steve Richmond, Rimbaud and Baudelaire, the spiritual brushes of a beautiful Rothko, the playfulness and intelligence of Basquiat and the honesty and starkness of Edward Hopper, the poems composed with the wonder and depth of Bach, the immediacy and daring of Stravinsky and the lush tenderness of Elgar: Hasta La Vista, Crazy is a superb collection of sentiment, outrage, gentleness, love, loss, regret, hope, humour and the confusion of common humanity, poems such as: 'A Cup Of Coffee' 'Cocaine Headaches' 'No Mas' 'Poem On Being 35' 'Telling The Truth' 'How Long Does It Take You To Write A Poem' 'A Bowl Of Pho' 'Flesh and Company' 'My Friend' 'The Promise' 'Coke Guilt' 'Hashtag That' will echo this firmly: Boski is a live-wire, he strikes elegantly with the power of Bruce Lee, he sings with the sad passion of Billie Holiday and his words dance with the grace and a style and a voice all of his very own: Boski has quickly become one of my favourite small press poets and he should be one of yours, buy this book and discover that for yourself.

- John D. Robinson: Poet & Publisher

David Boski is a poet after my own heart. A kindred spirit. A brother in arms. This is a collection of poems that will attack you from all angles, kick your teeth down your throat, and leave you with a toothless, bloody smile, begging for more. Tales of cocaine hangovers and questionable decisions, a study of the absurdity of existence and the madness of this thing we call life. A must-read book!

- Martin Appleby: Editor of Paper and Ink Literary Zine

DAVID BOSKI
HASTA LA VISTA, CRAZY

John D Robinson, author of "Pushing Away the Hours", presents his second book of poetry with Alien Buddha Press, "A HASH SMOKING, CODEINE SWALLOWING, WINE DRINKING SON OF A BITCH"

ISBN: 9781686391170

James Reitter is an Associate Professor of English and Film Studies and lives in Dutchess County, New York with his wife Ann and two cats. He is also an editor for Masque & Spectacle, an online journal devoted to writing and artwork.

Made in the
USA
Middletown, DE